What I Saw!
in Grand Teton

Text by Julie Gillum Lue   Photographs by Christopher Cauble

The Exploration of

_____

(Explorer, A.K.A. your name here)

/   /   to   /   /

(Dates of exploration)

RIVERBEND
PUBLISHING

What I Saw! in Grand Teton
© 2017 by Riverbend Publishing
Text by Julie Gillum Lue
Photographs by Christopher Cauble, www.caublephotography.com
Published by Riverbend Publishing, Helena, Montana

Design by Sarah Cauble, www.sarahcauble.com

ISBN 13: 978-1-60639-098-6

Printed in the United States of America

3 4 5 6 7 8 9 0 VP 25 24 23 22

Riverbend Publishing
P.O. Box 5833
Helena, MT 59604
1-866-787-2363
www.riverbendpublishing.com

Dedication

For Quinn, Jaren, and Tony

Acknowledgments

My thanks to Riverbend Publishing and Chris Cauble for giving me this opportunity, and to Durrae Johanek for her contributions from *What I Saw in Yellowstone*. I also would like to thank Frances Clark of the Wyoming Native Plant Society for help with wildflowers; wildlife researcher Andrew Jakes for answering my questions about pronghorn; elementary-school teacher Suzy Miller for insight and ideas for teachers; my son Quinn for editorial comments from a kid's perspective; and Andrew White and Andrew Langford of Grand Teton National Park for helping make the book more interesting and accurate. Any remaining errors can be blamed on me! I am also grateful to my parents for taking me and my sister camping in Grand Teton National Park nearly every year when we were kids. Some childhood experiences don't stick. Those did.

About the Author

Julie Gillum Lue grew up in the Colorado mountains, where she learned to love the outdoors and public lands. She graduated from the University of Colorado School of Journalism and also studied elementary education. After college she worked for the National Park Service for about eight years, mostly in Rocky Mountain and Canyonlands national parks. She later transferred to the US Fish & Wildlife Service and the US Forest Service. She now lives in Montana, where she writes about family and the outdoors. You may find her online at julielue.com.

★ ★ ★

About the Photographer

Christopher Cauble grew up in Montana, where he began his passion for photography by exploring the mountains with a 35mm film camera passed down from his parents. After graduating from the University of Montana, he became a freelance photographer working mostly in Montana and Yellowstone National Park. His work has been featured in magazines and books, including *Yellowstone: A Land of Wild and Wonder*, *A Montana Journal*, and the popular children's book, *What I Saw In Yellowstone*. Cauble is also a nature cinematographer and his videos have been published on many national and international news sites and television programs. He lives in Livingston, Montana. His work can be found at www.caublephotography.com and on social media.

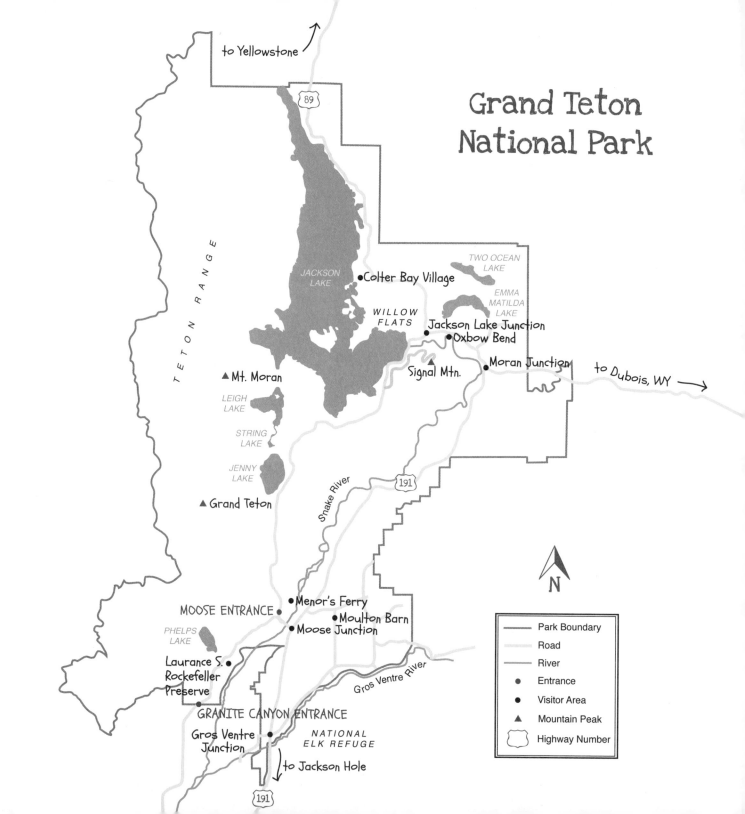

to Yellowstone

89

Grand Teton National Park

TWO OCEAN LAKE

JACKSON LAKE

•Colter Bay Village

WILLOW FLATS

EMMA MATILDA LAKE

Jackson Lake Junction
•Oxbow Bend

▲ Mt. Moran

Signal Mtn. ▲

Moran Junction

to Dubois, WY

LEIGH LAKE

STRING LAKE

TETON RANGE

JENNY LAKE

Snake River

191

▲ Grand Teton

N

MOOSE ENTRANCE

•Menor's Ferry

•Moulton Barn
•Moose Junction

PHELPS LAKE

Laurance S. Rockefeller Preserve

Gros Ventre River

GRANITE CANYON ENTRANCE

Gros Ventre Junction

NATIONAL ELK REFUGE

	Park Boundary
	Road
	River
●	Entrance
●	Visitor Area
▲	Mountain Peak
	Highway Number

to Jackson Hole

191

Contents

Introduction

When you think of Grand Teton National Park, do you picture mountains? Even before you first visited the park, you probably saw photographs of the Tetons. These jagged peaks, which tower over the valley called Jackson Hole in northwest Wyoming, are familiar to many people all over the world.

The Teton Range is easy to recognize because it looks so different from other mountain ranges. Earthquakes and glaciers helped create its unique shape. The mountains climb steeply from the valley, as if they have been pushed straight up through the plains. They are also pointed, like giant fangs. You can see why the Shoshone Indians named the Tetons "Teewinot," or "many pinnacles."

Each year, millions of visitors come to Grand Teton National Park to see these beautiful mountains.

Bull moose causing a "moose jam."

But mountains are just part of the story here. You will also find wildflower meadows, rivers, lakes, glaciers, and many kinds of animals—from bears and wolves to chipmunks and hummingbirds. Jackson Hole and the Teton Range have provided a home for people for at least 11,000 years. When fur trappers arrived in the early 1800s, they found the area being used by American Indians.

By the end of the century, settlers had started to build homesteads, cattle ranches, and dude ranches.

As more settlers arrived and wildlife started to disappear, some groups worried that this special place was being spoiled. They wanted a national park to preserve the area for future generations of people— like you! Grand Teton National Park was established in 1929 and enlarged in 1950. It now protects 310,000 acres of mostly wild land, an area about the size of Los Angeles with its almost four million people!

What I Saw in Grand Teton will help you learn about the animals, plants, and places you are most likely to see when visiting the park. But if this book included everything you could find, it might weigh more than you do! Some animals, like bighorn sheep, are not featured in the book because they are so difficult to see here. Others, like great horned owls, are nocturnal, which means they are active at night, when you are not.

As you travel through the park, see how many items in this book you can check off. Don't be disappointed if you can't find everything, especially the animals. The park is not a zoo. The animals roam where they please. If you don't see them, you can still learn about them, listen for their calls, and watch for their tracks or "scat" (a word biologists use for animal poop).

Chipmunk

Even when the animals are napping in the woods, the park has plenty for you to see and do. While you are exploring, ask your family to help you find answers to these questions:

★ How did the big boulders around Jenny and Taggart lakes get there?

★ How can you take a wagon across a river without a bridge?

★ How cold can it get in the park?

★ How do scientists know people have lived here for thousands of years?

★ What lake in the park has 15 islands?

GRAND TETON
NATIONAL PARK

The answers are in this book. But as you visit the park, you will come across things that are not in this book. If you find a plant or animal you can't identify, take a picture. Bring the picture to a visitor center and ask a ranger to identify it, or visit a park bookstore where you can find books on just about everything related to the park.

While having fun here, make sure you stay safe. Smart choices are your best defense against fast water, dangerous weather, wild animals, and other things that may hurt you. Please read the park newspaper for safety

Mount Moran

advice, including information on hiking and camping in bear country.

Here are a few rules you should follow to help protect you, the animals, and the park:

★ Stay at least 100 yards away from bears and wolves, and 25 yards away from other large animals.

★ Don't give any food to the animals. It's unhealthy for them and can be dangerous for you.

★ Leave flowers, plants, rocks, animals, and historic artifacts where they are.

Your best souvenirs are photos and memories, including the notes you make in this book. As you explore, maybe you'll be able to answer this question:

★ What is your favorite thing in Grand Teton National Park?

Bison calf

Moose

(Alces alces)

Where to see them

Watch for moose along the **Gros Ventre River** and the **Moose-Wilson Road**, and at **Oxbow Bend**, **Cottonwood Creek**, and **Willow Flats**. Sometimes you can even see moose in the **town of Moose**, near the **Snake River Bridge**.

Moose are the second-largest animals in Grand Teton National Park. Only bison are bigger. But moose don't let their size slow them down. Even when hauling around antlers that weigh more than 30 pounds, moose are amazing athletes ready to run, swim, dive, and fight.

Nothing else looks quite like a moose, with its long legs, horse-sized body, strangely shaped nose, and furry skin flap (called a "dewlap") hanging under its chin.

Like other members of the deer family, the males, called bulls, drop their antlers every winter and start re-growing them every spring. Scientists describe moose antlers as "palmate." Can you guess why? Each antler is shaped sort of like a hand. The females, called cows, have no antlers. In the spring, a cow moose gives birth to one or two cinnamon-colored calves.

Moose can run surprisingly fast—up to 35 miles per hour. Their long legs help them wade through deep snow in winter and step over fallen trees in the forest. Moose also use their powerful legs and hooves to defend themselves. Sometimes a single moose can fight off an entire wolf pack!

In summer, you are likely to find moose cooling off or feeding in rivers or ponds. They can eat plants growing underwater by closing their nostrils. Moose can swim for miles and even dive under water almost 20 feet to snag a tasty plant.

Unlike elk and bison, moose don't form herds. You usually see a lone moose, or maybe a cow with a calf. Watch for moose where you see water and willows, one of their favorite foods.

Cow moose

It's exciting to see a moose, but don't forget to keep your distance. Moose can be dangerous if they feel threatened.

Guess What?

Moose probably didn't move into Grand Teton National Park until around 1900. Now there are about 500 moose living in the park and surrounding areas.

Bull moose

☐ I saw a moose!

Where?

When?

What was it doing?

Cow moose and her calf

Bison

(Bison bison)

Where to see them

Look for bison in the park's grasslands and sagebrush flats, especially along the **Kelly-Antelope Flats Loop**. The bison herd moves with the seasons, so ask at the visitor center about recent sightings.

Almost a thousand bison live in the park during the summer, and sometimes you can see them from the roads. But don't approach them. Many people have been hurt by bison when trying to get too close, usually to take a picture!

If you call a bison a buffalo, everyone will know what you mean. But scientifically speaking, true buffalo and bison are not the same.

A full-grown bison can weigh 2,000 pounds. You might think such a large animal would be slow, but bison can run more than 30 miles per hour, faster than any person. Both male and female bison have thick horns and long, dense hair on their heads and shoulders. When calves are born in April and May, they have reddish-brown fur (see page 7). Some people call them "red dogs." As they get older, the calves turn dark brown like their parents.

Bison are grazers and prefer grasses and similar plants. In winter, they swing their shaggy heads back and forth to sweep away snow so they can reach the grass beneath it. Most of the bison leave the park each winter and travel to the nearby National Elk Refuge, where food is more available.

Huge herds of bison used to rumble across the West, but all except for a few hundred were killed. No bison roamed the park from the mid-1800s until 1968, when 15 escaped from the Jackson Hole Wildlife Park.

Guess what?

Bison are North America's largest land animals. One bison can weigh as much as a moose and a grizzly combined.

☐ I saw bison!

Where?

When?

How many?

What were they doing?

Pronghorn

(Antilocapra americana)

Sometimes pronghorn are called antelope, but they are not really antelope. The pronghorn's closest living relative is the giraffe! Still, if you see a place with "antelope" in its name, watch for pronghorn.

Pronghorn are a little smaller than deer and often can be found grazing peacefully on sagebrush flats or open hillsides. But if pronghorn sense danger, they can sprint away at 45 miles per hour and keep going for miles. Even a week-old baby pronghorn, called a fawn, could outrun you.

Male pronghorn have "pronged," or forked, horns about a foot long. The females have tiny horns more like nubs. Animals with horns (not antlers) usually keep them year-round. Pronghorn are different because they shed the outer covering of their horns every fall and start to regrow it in the winter.

Pronghorn have special fur with hollow hairs to help them stay warm in cold weather. But in winter, they still need to migrate to areas with less snow so they can reach their food. Pronghorn herds in Grand Teton National Park leave each winter and travel more than 150 miles to the Upper Green River Basin, where they will stay until returning to the park in the spring. Sometimes they run into trouble when their route is blocked by fences. Unlike deer, pronghorn don't jump very well and almost never try to jump over fences. They prefer to slip under the bottom of a fence if there is room.

☐ I saw pronghorn!

Where?

When?

How many?

What were they doing?

Guess What?

The pronghorn is the second-fastest land mammal in the world. In a short race, it would lose only to a cheetah. In a longer race with a cheetah, it might win, as cheetahs get tired faster.

(Cervus elaphus)

Where to see them

In summer, you may see elk near **Timbered Island**, **North Jenny Lake**, **Willow Flats**, or the **Blacktail Ponds Overlook**. You may also see them along the road north of **Jackson Lake**. In winter, look for elk outside the park at the **National Elk Refuge**.

In the fall, you might hear an elk before you see it. A male elk, called a bull, "bugles" to challenge other bulls and let females know he is available for breeding. The bugle is a loud call that starts low and rises until it ends in a long, high-pitched squeal, often followed by several grunts. If another bull takes up the challenge, the two bulls may spar with their heavy antlers.

While a bull's antlers are re-growing each year, they are covered with "velvet"—a layer of skin and short hairs that is later scraped off. A pair of antlers from a grown bull elk can measure five feet across. Young bulls with skinny, unbranched antlers are called "spike bulls."

Elk form different kinds of herds depending on the time of year. In summer, older bulls often form small herds of their own. Cows, their spotted calves, and other young elk form larger herds. In the fall, the most dominant bulls guard groups of cows from other males.

Though elk like to feed in meadows, they go into forests to rest, hide, or take shelter from bad weather. When winter comes, most of the elk leave the park and go to the National Elk Refuge. It was created in 1912 to give elk a place to live and feed in the winter, after they lost much of their winter range to homes and ranches.

Bull elk

Guess what?

Another name for elk is wapiti, a Shawnee word pronounced WAH-pit-ee. It means "white rump," and when you see an elk you'll know why.

☐ **I saw elk!**

Where?

When?

How many?

What were they doing?

Where to see them

You may find mule deer just about anywhere, but watch for them along the **Moose-Wilson Road**, near **Timbered Island**, around **Colter Bay**, or in meadows along the road north of **Jackson Lake**.

Mule Deer

(Odocoileus hemionus)

If you see a deer in Grand Teton National Park, it's probably a mule deer. White-tailed deer are not as common here. Mule deer are bigger than white-tails and have short tails with black tips. Their name refers to their large ears, which look like the ears of a mule. The males, known as bucks, grow antlers that branch into forks and then divide again (like factor trees in fourth-grade math).

"Muleys" can gallop at around 40 miles per hour. But when they are startled, they often bounce

Mule deer buck

Mule deer doe

away with all of their legs springing up and down at the same time, like a four-legged pogo stick: *boing-boing-boing.* This unusual gait, called "stotting," is used to escape danger. In the park, deer have to be alert for many predators, including mountain lions.

Mule deer eat aspens and other trees, shrubs, grasses, flowering plants, and mushrooms. They are more likely to be out feeding in the morning and late evening. At other times of day, watch for their heart-shaped tracks in soft ground or the mud along streams. You may find the tiny hoof prints of fawns mixed with those of their mothers, which are known as does.

☐ I saw mule deer!

Where?

When?

How many?

What were they doing?

Guess What?

Mule deer are great jumpers. While stotting, they can cover 15 or 20 feet of ground with a single bound, and they can easily jump fences of six feet or more.

Coyote

(Canis latrans)

Where to see them

Look for coyotes in open areas like those along the **Antelope Flats-Kelly Loop** or the **Moose-Wilson Road**.

Of the three types of wild dogs in the park—wolves, coyotes, and foxes—you are most likely to see a coyote. Coyotes are more active at night, but sometimes you can find them hunting during the day, especially when they have hungry pups to feed.

Coyotes mostly hunt for voles, mice, ground squirrels, rabbits, and other small animals. When a coyote sees a mouse, it springs into the air and pounces like a cat. Coyotes also sneak around carcasses of animals that wolves have killed, hoping to dash in and grab a bite to eat without being caught. But they usually avoid wolves. Wolves may attack and kill coyotes.

An adult coyote is as tall as a medium-sized dog and weighs about 25 to 35 pounds. Coyotes usually have grayish-brown coats and big, bushy tails. Wolves are much taller, more than twice as heavy, and have fur in a variety of colors, from almost white to black.

In the spring, a coyote mother gives birth to four or more pups in an underground den. Both parents bring food to them until the pups are big enough to travel.

Coyotes can be quiet and stealthy while hunting. But they can also make a lot of noise, especially at night. They bark, yip, yowl, and howl. Their calls sound very different from a wolf's long, deep, steady howl.

Guess What?

You may pronounce this animal's name as a three-syllable word, ky-O-tee, or with two syllables, KYE-ote. Most people in this area say KYE-ote.

☐ I saw a coyote!

Where?

When?

What was it doing?

Where to see them

Watch for beavers along the **Snake River**, at **Oxbow Bend**, or at **Willow Flats**. You can find beaver dams at **Schwabacher Landing** and along the **Moose-Wilson Road**.

Beaver

(Castor canadensis)

If you are walking by a stream or pond and hear a loud splash, you may have just startled a beaver. Beavers slap their wide, flattened tails against the water to warn others of danger. After sounding the alarm, beavers may dive and stay underwater a long time—up to 15 minutes!

These large, furry, brown rodents grow up to 50 pounds or more. They do most of their work at night, but sometimes you can catch beavers out for a swim in the early morning or late evening. Their webbed hind feet serve as swim flippers, and oil from a special gland keeps their thick, soft fur warm and dry.

Beavers build dams to create areas with deep, calm water where they can raise their families and store food for winter. You may find stumps of trees that were cut down by beavers. They gnaw away the wood with their large front teeth until the tree falls over. Then they eat the tender smaller branches and use other branches for building their dams and lodges. To build a dam, they weave together tree limbs and mud. Their lodge (home) looks like a rounded haystack of sticks and branches.

Beavers help create habitats (places to live) for other wildlife like muskrats, frogs, and ducks. Muskrats look a bit like tiny beavers but with slimmer, "rattier" tails.

PHOTO BY CINDY GOEDDEL

☐ I saw a beaver!

Where?

When?

What was it doing?

Guess What?

Beavers have clear inner eyelids they can close underwater to protect their eyes—kind of like built-in swim goggles.

15

Grizzly Bear

(Ursus arctos)

When grizzly cubs are born, they weigh about as much as a football. But by the time they leave their mother two or three years later, they will be almost as big as she is. As adults, grizzlies weigh up to twice as much as black bears. Male grizzlies in this area sometimes reach 700 pounds.

Grizzly bears eat meat when they can get it, and they often feed on carcasses of animals that have died over the winter. But they also eat enormous amounts of plants and insects. Sometimes you can find areas where grizzlies have tipped over rocks and torn up the ground while digging for roots, bulbs, and grubs. They rip through the soil with sharp, curved claws that can grow longer than your fingers.

You probably already know that bears like berries. But you might be surprised by some of a grizzly's other favorite foods, which include army cutworm moths, whitebark pine seeds, cutthroat trout, elk, and ladybugs.

Like marmots and ground squirrels, grizzlies hibernate each winter. But bears' bodies don't get as cold as other hibernating animals, and bears can wake up much more easily.

Even though grizzly bears are not easy to find, you still need to be prepared to come across one almost anywhere. Make sure you read the latest information from the National Park Service about staying safe around bears.

Guess What?

The grizzly bear is sometimes called a "silvertip" because the tips of its long hairs are light-colored or silvery. Another word for this coloration is "grizzled," which gives us the bear's name, "grizzly."

☐ I saw a grizzly bear!

Where?

When?

What was it doing?

Where to see them

You may see black bears in **Cascade** or **Death canyons**, along the **Moose-Wilson** or **Signal Mountain Summit roads**, or at **Two Ocean** and **Emma Matilda lakes**.

Black Bear

(Ursus americanus)

Black bears share the park with grizzly bears, but they don't want to run into a grizzly any more than humans do. Grizzlies are larger and more powerful and may even kill black bears.

To tell a black bear from a grizzly, look at rumps and humps. When a black bear stands on all four feet, its rump is a little taller than its shoulders. A grizzly bear's rump is lower than the big hump on its shoulders.

If you are lucky enough to see a black bear, it may be gorging on berries or cracking open a log, looking for grubs and insects. Black bears mostly feed on plants. They love dandelions! But they will eat almost anything, including fish, elk calves, ants, and bees. They will also eat your food if you are not careful. It's important to never leave food where bears can reach it. Bears that learn to eat human food get into trouble, and they usually have to be killed.

Black bears are active from spring through fall. In the winter, they head to their dens and enter a deep sleep called hibernation. Females give birth to tiny cubs while still in their dens. The new family leaves the den in spring when the cubs are big enough to start exploring. Black bears are great climbers, and even the cubs can shimmy up a tree in seconds when they are scared.

☐ I saw a black bear!

Where?

When?

What was it doing?

Guess What?

Not all black bears are black. Their fur varies from almost blond to cinnamon to brown to black.

Red Squirrel

(Tamiasciurus hudsonicus)

Where to see them
You can find red squirrels in forested areas of the park, including those around **Jenny Lake**, **Colter Bay**, and **Two Ocean** and **Emma Matilda lakes**.

If you get too close to a red squirrel, it chatters loudly and lets out a squirrel yell that is hard to ignore. The red squirrel is very territorial. Not only will it chase other squirrels that come too close, it will chatter at any intruder, including you.

Red squirrels look more brown than red and have a ring of white around each eye. They are smaller than the gray squirrels and fox squirrels common in other places.

Because red squirrels don't hibernate, they must store food for the winter and keep it safe from

other animals. They eat a variety of food but mostly rely on seeds from pine, fir, and spruce cones. Red squirrels store their cones in piles called middens, which also serve as trash heaps for cones they have already chewed into bits.

Guess what?
Grizzly bears sometimes raid the middens of red squirrels to eat whitebark pine seeds.

☐ I saw a red squirrel!

Where?

When?

What was it doing?

Where to see them

You can see chipmunks almost anywhere in the park, from **sagebrush flats** to **alpine meadows**. They are often found at developed areas like campgrounds, picnic areas, and turnouts.

Chipmunk

(Tamias species)

Unless you visit the park in the middle of winter, you'll probably see a chipmunk or two—or more! You might see one run across a road or scurry along a trail. Chipmunks are curious and sometimes approach people, but don't try to touch them or feed them. As cute as they are, chipmunks can bite or spread diseases, and human food is not healthy for them.

Chipmunks are small members of the squirrel family. They are reddish-brown with long, bushy tails and thin white and black stripes on their backs and pointy faces.

These tiny rodents hardly ever sit still unless they pause for a snack. Chipmunks eat seeds, nuts, berries, insects, and sometimes eggs or baby birds. When they find food that won't spoil, they stuff it into their fur-lined cheek pouches to carry back home. A chipmunk spends winter in its nest, saving energy by lowering its body temperature in a kind of light hibernation. It wakes up regularly to eat some of the food it has stored.

☐ I saw a chipmunk!

Where?

When?

What was it doing?

Guess what?

When alarmed, the chipmunk gives a sharp call that sounds like "chip"—a good bet that's how it got its name.

19

Golden-Mantled Ground Squirrel

(Callospermophilus lateralis)

Where to see them

You can find golden-mantled ground squirrels at **Inspiration Point** above **Jenny Lake**, and in other rocky areas in the canyons at the base of the **Teton Range**.

You may have seen a golden-mantled ground squirrel without knowing it. Many people mistake these small, striped rodents for chipmunks. But you can easily tell the two species apart if you look at their heads. A chipmunk has stripes on its head and face, leading all the way to its pointed nose. A golden-mantled ground squirrel has no stripes on its head. The ground squirrels also are bigger and chubbier-looking.

Like chipmunks, golden-mantled ground squirrels pack food into their cheeks and haul it off to their burrows for storage. But they also eat enough to build up a thick fat layer. They spend the winter in hibernation and probably save most of their stored food for when they wake up in the spring.

Golden-mantled ground squirrels live in rocky areas in the

mountains. They may "beg" for food from you, but please resist. Feeding ground squirrels is bad for them and ruins your chance to see them acting naturally.

Guess What?

When they hibernate, golden-mantled ground squirrels lower their body temperature to near freezing!

☐ I saw a golden-mantled ground squirrel!

Where?

When?

What was it doing?

Where to see them

Watch for Uinta ground squirrels along **Mormon Row** and **Antelope Flats Road**, especially near the **Mormon Row** barns, and in the meadows near **Colter Bay**.

Uinta Ground Squirrel

(Urocitellus armatus)

While traveling through the sagebrush flats, watch for mounds of dirt marking the burrows of Uinta ground squirrels. You might find a Uinta ground squirrel scampering around or standing next to a burrow entrance, watching for danger. These ground squirrels need to stay alert because they are eaten by many predators, including coyotes, foxes, badgers, hawks, and eagles.

Uinta ground squirrels only see two seasons: spring and summer. They don't store food in their burrows. Instead, they store energy on their bodies in the form of a thick layer of fat. After eating and eating until they store up enough fat, they hibernate for the rest of the year. Sometimes they start as early as mid-summer! If you walk through the sagebrush in late summer, fall, or winter, think about the Uinta ground squirrels sleeping somewhere below in their grass-lined nests.

☐ **I saw an Uinta ground squirrel!**

Where?

When?

What was it doing?

Guess what?

Uinta ground squirrels hibernate for about seven or eight months—more than half the year.

Bald Eagle

(Haliaeetus leucocephalus)

Where to see them

Watch for eagles along the **Snake River** (including **Oxbow Bend**), **Gros Ventre River**, and **Jackson Lake**.

If you have ever seen a bald eagle, you know it's not really bald. The "bald" part of its name comes from an old English word that means white. Only adult birds have white heads and tails. Until they are around five years old, bald eagles are mostly dark brown with a few white feathers here and there. The young birds also have black beaks, which eventually turn yellow.

Bald eagles are large birds of prey, standing nearly three feet tall. When extended, their wings span six to seven feet. Because bald eagles mostly eat fish, you often see them perched on a tall tree at the edge of a river or lake. When an eagle sees a fish near the surface, it flies down to grab it with its sharp talons (claws).

Though bald eagles can catch their own fish, they steal it when they can. An eagle will ambush an osprey that has just caught a fish. The eagle swoops at the osprey, forcing it to drop the fish, or even snatches the fish directly from the osprey's talons. Bald eagles also kill ducks and other animals and eat carrion (dead animals).

About a dozen pairs of bald eagles nest in the park each year along the Snake River and the shores of Jackson Lake. They lay their eggs in late winter or early spring, when snow is still on the ground.

Guess What?

An eagle's nest can be 13 feet tall and weigh nearly a ton. It is often used year after year.

☐ I saw a bald eagle!

Where?

When?

What was it doing?

Where to See them

You can find ospreys along the **Snake River** (including **Oxbow Bend**), **Jackson Lake**, and **Two Ocean** and **Emma Matilda lakes**.

Osprey

(Pandion haliaetus)

Like bald eagles, ospreys eat fish, so you usually find them near water. You can see ospreys flying above rivers or lakes, perched on trees at water's edge, or sit-

ting on their nests. They are smaller than eagles and in flight their wings bend or "kink" backwards, instead of extending straight out.

Ospreys eat almost nothing but fish. They hunt by spotting fish from the air. Sometimes an osprey will hover briefly in one place, watching and waiting. When it sees a fish, the osprey dives from the sky. Just before entering the water, the osprey swings its feet forward so it can grab the slippery, squirming fish with its sharp talons and the spiny pads on its feet.

Successful or not, the wet bird rises from the water and flies away, usually pausing in midair to shake off water. On average, an osprey catches one fish for every four dives. When it catches one, the osprey will adjust its grip so the fish's head points forward, in the same direction the bird is flying. This makes the fish easier to carry.

An osprey takes the fish to a perch to eat, or to its nest to feed its young. Ospreys build their nests of sticks at the top of a tree or even a power pole. Many nests are used every year. Ospreys leave the park in the fall, heading south for warmer weather and "open" water (lakes and rivers that have not frozen over).

☐ I saw an osprey!

Where?

When?

What was it doing?

Guess What?

The osprey can dive up to three feet into the water to catch a fish.

23

Trumpeter Swan

(Cygnus buccinator)

Where to see them

You may see swans at **Oxbow Bend**, **Swan Lake**, or on the ponds by the **Moose-Wilson Road**. You might also find them on **Flat Creek** at the **National Elk Refuge**.

With their huge bodies and white feathers, trumpeter swans are easy to spot on a pond or lake. But to make sure you're not looking at pelicans instead, check out their bills. Trumpeter swans have short, slim, black bills. Pelicans have long, bulky, yellow-orange bills with a pouch for catching fish.

Trumpeters are among the heaviest birds in the world that can fly. They can weigh up to 30 pounds—more than California condors—and have wingspans of up to eight feet. Even their eggs are enormous. Each egg weighs about five times as much as a chicken egg.

Trumpeter swans often nest on a beaver lodge or small island in the middle of a pond or shallow lake. Baby swans, called cygnets (pronounced SIG-nets), are usually fluffy and gray—like the "ugly duckling" you may have read about in fairy tales. The cygnets will turn mostly white by the end of their first year.

A hundred years ago, you would have been unlikely to see any trumpeter swans. People hunted them for their beautiful feathers, and very few trumpeters were

left in the world. Now the swans are protected, and their populations have increased. You may be lucky enough to see them or hear their strange, trumpeting calls.

Guess What?

Trumpeters like a long "runway" of open water for taking off—about the same length as a football field.

☐ I saw a trumpeter swan!

Where?

When?

What was it doing?

24

Where to see them

Great blue herons can be found almost anywhere there is water, but you are especially likely to see them in the quiet waters of **Oxbow Bend**, along other parts of the **Snake River**, and at beaver ponds like those at **Schwabacher Landing** or along the **Moose-Wilson Road**.

Whenever you are near water, watch for great blue herons "spearfishing" in the shallows. Great blues, as they are sometimes called, are tall, bluish-gray birds with black crests. They have long, slim necks they can curve into an S shape, almost like a snake ready to strike.

Great blue herons wade quietly in shallow water, watching for a chance to snatch up or stab a meal with their sharp bills. If you are patient, you might be able to see one catch a fish. Great blues also eat frogs, mice, and just about any other small creatures they can swallow.

Sometimes people confuse great blue herons with sandhill cranes. Both birds are tall and have long, pointed bills. But when the birds fly, it is easy to tell them apart. Great blue herons fold their necks back over their shoulders. Sandhill cranes stretch their necks out full length. Cranes also call frequently, making a sound like a rattle. Herons are more quiet, and when they do make a call, it sounds like a loud, hoarse croak.

Even when you don't see herons, look for their huge tracks in the mud near the edges of streams or ponds. Heron tracks are about six inches long, with one toe in back and three unevenly spaced toes in front.

☐ I saw a great blue heron!

Where?

When?

What was it doing?

Guess what?

Great blue herons like to nest in colonies (called rookeries) with other herons—sometimes hundreds of them. The biggest rookery in the park has about 20 nests.

25

Gray Jay

(Perisoreus canadensis)

If you have a picnic in the woods, you might learn why some people call gray jays "camp robbers." These cute, fluffy birds often flutter silently to nearby trees, ready to swoop in and steal a bite of your lunch. But please do not feed them. Gray jays rely on food they gather in the summer to live through the coming winter. Human food may not give them what they need to survive.

Gray jays hide food throughout their territories with the help of a special tool—extra-sticky saliva (yes, that's spit). When a gray jay finds a berry it wants to store for winter, it works the berry around in its mouth until it is well-coated and then "glues" it under a piece of bark or a branch. The gray jay stores, or caches, thousands of berries, insects, and other bits of food this way. Amazingly, it remembers where to find them months later when there is little else to eat.

This cache of food scattered throughout the forest lets gray jays live in places that most birds leave in the

winter. It also allows them to build nests and lay eggs in late winter in temperatures down to -20 degrees Fahrenheit! Gray jays keep their babies fed and warm in nests built of twigs, insulated with cocoons, and lined with feathers and animal fur.

Guess What?
Gray jays can lift two-thirds of their body weight and carry food with their feet, as well as their beaks.

☐ I saw a gray jay!

Where?

When?

What was it doing?

Where to See them

Watch for bluebirds in mountain meadows and **sagebrush flats**, especially in the area around **Antelope Flats** and **Mormon Row**.

Mountain Bluebird

(Sialia currucoides)

Mountain bluebirds wear the colors of the sky. Males are bright blue on top and lighter blue underneath. Females are mostly soft gray with just a touch of blue. Watch for them flitting across meadows and sagebrush flats, or perched on fence posts and treetops.

Bluebirds nest in cavities—another name for holes. But with their small bills, bluebirds cannot excavate their own homes. Outside the park, they often nest in birdhouses built by people. Inside the park, bluebirds nest in cavities drilled out by woodpeckers in old cottonwood or aspen trees. They usually choose a nesting site with a good view of a meadow or other open area where they can hunt.

Mountain bluebirds like to eat caterpillars, grasshoppers, beetles, and spiders. When hunting, they look more like tiny birds of prey than songbirds. They hover above the ground like miniature helicopters or even catch bugs in midair. When they can, bluebirds watch from a fencepost or treetop and swoop down when they see something within range. They need to save energy, because after their eggs hatch, they will deliver food to their babies about a dozen times an hour.

During the breeding season, bluebirds are territorial. They won't allow other bluebirds to nest within a hundred yards or so. Once babies have grown, they will often join larger flocks in the fall.

☐ I saw a mountain bluebird!

Where?

When?

What was it doing?

Guess What?

Bluebird feathers do not contain any blue pigments. The birds look blue because of the way tiny air pockets in their feathers reflect light—something called "structural coloration."

27

Arrowleaf Balsamroot

Where to see them
Arrowleaf balsamroot blooms early to mid-summer in **sagebrush flats** and on open hillsides throughout the valley.

(Balsamorhiza sagittata)

Arrowleaf balsamroot gets the first part of its common name from its leaves. They are shaped like large, fuzzy arrowheads. The second part of its name comes from its roots, which smell like a balsam fir tree. Native American tribes used most parts of the plant for food or medicine.

Balsamroot is a wild sunflower. It sends up stalks and leaves from low clumps. In late spring, each stalk produces a yellow flower that looks like a daisy. You might see

acres and acres of these yellow flowers blooming in one area, especially on hillsides. Deer and elk like to eat balsamroot. You often find plants or flowers that have been munched.

Look for balsamroot and other wildflowers near Lupine Meadows, North Blacktail Butte, Two Ocean and Emma Matilda lakes, the Antelope Flats-Kelly Loop, and the Moose-Wilson Road.

Guess What?
Arrowleaf balsamroot's huge taproot—up to eight feet long and four inches across—allows it to survive most fires. After a fire, the plant regrows from its roots.

☐ I saw arrowleaf balsamroot!
Where?

When?

What was it like?

28

Where to see them

Look for lupine in sagebrush areas and meadows, including **Lupine Meadows**.

Lupine

(Lupinus species)

In a flower garden, you can find lupines (pronounced LOO-pins) blooming in almost any color. But in the park, wild lupines shoot up spikes of blue and purple flowers. A lupine's flowers bloom on all sides of a tall, straight stem. Its leaves look like green starbursts, with long leaflets (parts of the leaf) growing out from a common center. After a rain or heavy dew, you can find drops of water trapped in the centers of these starbursts.

Lupines are legumes, related to peas, beans, and peanuts. Their seeds look like small, oval peas in a pod.

Don't eat them. Some lupines are poisonous. Like other legumes, lupines have special nodules (bumps) on their roots that help the plant take nitrogen out of the air and make it available in the soil, which helps plants to grow.

☐ I saw lupine!

Where?

When?

What was it like?

Guess what?

Lupine is a Latin word that means "wolf-like." People used to think lupines gobbled up all the minerals and other nutrients in the soil.

Skyrocket

Where to See them

Skyrocket grows in dry places with plenty of sun, from **sagebrush flats** to **mountain meadows**.

(Ipomopsis aggregata)

Skyrocket has many common names, including scarlet gilia, fairy trumpet, and hummingbird flower. Its bright, red-orange flowers bloom on a tall stem covered with leaves as skinny as pine needles.

Hummingbirds love skyrocket. A hummer's long bill and tongue fit perfectly down the flower's trumpet-shaped tube to reach a drop of nectar. As the hummingbird drinks the nectar, tiny grains of pollen on its feathers get transferred from one skyrocket to another, helping to pollinate the flowers.

If you find a patch of skyrocket in the park, you may see broad-tailed or calliope hummingbirds buzzing from flower to flower. Calliopes are very small. Each bird weighs about as much as a penny! You may also see a creature that looks like a hummingbird but with a beaky-looking proboscis that bends in the middle. This insect, called a hawk moth, likes skyrocket too.

Guess What?

Skyrocket is also called "skunk flower." The leaves at its base have a skunky smell, which attracts insects.

☐ I Saw Skyrocket!

Where?

When?

What was it like?

Where to See them

You can find sticky geranium putting on a show in the valley and its paler relative, Richardson's geranium, blooming higher up in the canyons.

Wild Geranium

(Geranium species)

Wild geranium is sometimes called cranesbill. After a flower dies away, the plant produces a "fruit" or seed capsule that looks like the head of a bird with a long bill—perhaps a crane. When the seed capsule dries out, it pops open and the seeds go flying.

Two kinds of wild geranium grow in the park. Sticky geranium, with dark pink flowers, has leaves covered with sticky hairs, possibly to protect it from crawling insects. Some scientists call sticky geranium a "protocarnivore." It has the

ability to digest (eat) proteins in these insects! Richardson's geranium blooms white or light pink. Both kinds have darker lines on their flowers, known as nectar guides, that help direct bees and other pollinators to their favorite food.

Richardson's geranium

Sticky geranium

☐ I saw a wild geranium!

Where?

When?

What was it like?

Guess What?

Wildflowers are an important part of the park's ecosystem. They provide food for many animals, from delicate butterflies to massive grizzly bears. Enjoy their beauty, but please don't pick the flowers.

Big Sagebrush

(Artemisia tridentata)

Most people recognize sagebrush, a shrub with scratchy, twisted branches and soft, silvery green leaves. In the park, big sagebrush is one of the most common

plants. Though it usually grows to about waist-high, in some areas it can grow much bigger. When you pinch a leaf, it gives off a sharp smell, kind of like medicine.

In some ways, an area covered with sagebrush is like a very short forest. Sagebrush plants serve as the "trees." They protect smaller plants from sun and wind. They also pull up water with their deep taproots, making it more available in the soil. For animals, sagebrush provides shelter, food, and a place to nest.

Some animals can't eat much sagebrush without getting sick. Others, like pronghorn, eat plenty of it, especially in winter. They must not mind the smell!

When traveling through sagebrush country, watch for large animals like pronghorn and coyotes and smaller animals like badgers, ground squirrels, meadowlarks, and greater-sage grouse.

Greater-sage grouse rely on sagebrush for almost everything, including food, cover, and a place to nest and raise their babies. For them, nothing is more welcoming than miles and miles of sage. In summer, sage grouse are hard to find. But if you visit the park in spring, you might see groups of male greater-sage grouse putting on a show to impress the females.

Guess what?
Big sagebrush can live more than a hundred years.

☐ I saw big sagebrush!

Where?

When?

What was it like?

Where to see them

Aspens grow in meadows and on mountainsides throughout the park. Fall colors are especially nice at **Oxbow Bend** and along the **Moose-Wilson Road**.

Aspen

(Populus tremuloides)

Aspens are closely related to cottonwoods, another tree you are likely to see in the park. But telling them apart is easy if you look at their bark. Aspens have smooth, whitish-green bark that shows every past injury with a black scar. Cottonwoods have thick, rough bark with furrows deep enough to hold your fingers. The leaves on both trees turn a bright yellow-gold in the fall.

Aspens are sometimes called "quakies" because of the way their leaves quiver in a breeze. The stems of most tree leaves are round, but the aspen's leaf stems are flattened, like a circle squashed into an oval. When the wind blows, the flattened stem causes the leaf to tremble and flutter, or "quake." See for yourself—blow gently on a leaf and watch it twist and turn. Aspen leaves are a little lighter in color on one side, making the fluttering more obvious.

Even though aspens produce seeds, most new trees grow as sprouts from the roots of an existing tree. This means that aspen trees growing in the same area may actually be parts of the same tree.

Aspen groves provide a place to nest for many birds and food for many animals. Elk and moose often eat the leaves and small twigs on young aspens. In winter, they scrape off the bark of older trees with their teeth.

☐ I saw aspens!

Where?

When?

How many?

What were they like?

Guess what?

A grove of aspens that share a root system is called a "clone" or "clonal colony." In the fall, aspens in a clonal colony turn the same color at the same time.

Lodgepole Pine

(Pinus contorta)

Where to see them

You can find lodgepole pines growing in most of the lower parts of the park. Look for them on the moraines surrounding **Jenny** and **Jackson lakes**.

If you see a forest of tall, skinny conifers topped by clumps of branches, you're probably looking at lodgepole pines. When lodgepoles grow in a crowd, their lower trunks are mostly bare. When they have plenty of space, they grow in more of a bushy pyramid shape with plenty of lower branches. To be sure you're looking at a lodgepole, check the tree's needles—the lodgepole is the only pine in this area with needles in bunches of two.

Lodgepole pines are the most common tree in the park. They often grow on moraines (ridges of rocks and dirt pushed up by glaciers) like the ones surrounding Jenny Lake. These moraines hold more nutrients and water than the surrounding flat ground.

Lodgepole forests bounce back quickly after forest fires, even when many trees are killed. They drop pinecones full of seeds each year, but the topmost pinecones stay on the trees. These cones are sealed shut with sticky pine resin. When the heat from a fire melts the resin, these cones open up, spilling out their seeds. The fire burns out, but millions of lodgepole seeds lie on the ground. Many of these will successfully sprout into new trees.

Guess What?

Native Americans in the Rocky Mountains used—and sometimes still use—poles from lodgepole pines for their tipis, or lodges. That's why these trees are called lodgepole pines.

☐ I saw lodgepole pines!

Where?

When?

How many?

What were they like?

Where to See it

From most of the southern part of the park, with especially nice views of the peak from the **Mountain View** turnout, and a good view of the **Teton Fault** from the **Cathedral Group** turnout.

Grand Teton is the name of both the national park and its tallest mountain. When you stand on the valley floor, the summit of this mountain looms more than 7,000 feet above your head. That's well over a mile, or about six times the height of the Empire State Building.

But you won't find any elevators leading to the top of Grand Teton. Reaching the summit is hard work. It also requires special skills and climbing equipment, including ropes. Climbers must cope with sheer drops, steep snowfields,

and severe weather like lightning or even avalanches. Fortunately, you don't need to climb Grand Teton to appreciate the forces that helped create it.

The elevation at the summit is already 13,770 feet above sea level. But Grand Teton and the rest of the Teton Range probably will grow even taller. The Teton Fault—a giant crack in the ground, where two pieces of the earth's crust rub against each other—runs for about 40 miles along the east edge of the mountains. Every few thousand years, a huge earthquake, up to 7.5 magnitude, shakes this fault. Each earthquake shoves the Teton Range a little higher while dropping the valley a little lower. The Teton Fault hasn't had a big earthquake in a long time, but scientists expect it will happen again.

☐ I saw Grand Teton!

When?

What was it like?

Guess what?

Grand Teton is a "glacial horn" like the Matterhorn in Europe. Its pyramid shape was carved by glaciers, which once surrounded it on all sides.

Teton Glacier

Where to see it

From the **Teton Glacier** turnout, about halfway between **Moose** and **Jenny Lake**.

Even in the middle of summer, you can see a large patch of white on the north side of Grand Teton. This patch is Teton Glacier, the biggest glacier still left in the park from the "Little Ice Age," which ended almost 200 years ago.

Teton Glacier, at around 50 acres, is tiny compared to the giant glaciers that covered this area during the true Ice Ages. Even Jackson Hole was buried under more than a thousand feet of ice. By the time the last of this ice melted, about 14,000 years ago, it had changed almost everything.

Glaciers form when snow gets deeper and deeper each winter and does not melt too much over the summer. When it gets deep enough, the snow's own weight squashes it into glacial ice. Then the ice starts to flow downhill, like a slow but very powerful river. As it moves, the ice grinds away at whatever is in its path and carries it along.

Even though the most massive glaciers are long gone from the Tetons, you can find signs of them everywhere. They carved the jagged shapes of the Teton Range, bulldozed the U-shaped canyons, and excavated

the lakes at the base of the mountains. As they moved, glaciers pushed up ridges of dirt and rock, called moraines, along their sides and front. They also carried and later dropped large boulders, some as big as cars.

Guess What?

Teton Glacier and the rest of glaciers in the park are disappearing. The Teton Range gets about 40 feet of snow each winter, but warm summers have been melting away more snow.

☐ I saw Teton Glacier!

When?

What was it like?

Jenny Lake offers a bit of everything: a visitor center, ranger station, campground, and trailhead. You can even reach some popular hiking areas by way of a special shortcut—across the lake! For a fee, you can ride a shuttle boat across Jenny Lake to the trail for Hidden Falls, Inspiration Point, and Cascade Canyon. If you don't want to take the boat, you can still reach these areas by hiking the trail that follows the lakeshore.

While exploring the Jenny Lake area, you can see evidence of past glaciers in the U shape of Cascade Canyon, the deep pit that holds the lake, and the lodgepole-covered moraines (ridges) that surround it. You can also find boulders, called glacial erratics, that hitched a ride on glaciers and were left behind when the ice melted.

Watch for these glacial erratics when walking around Jenny or Taggart lakes or the Jenny Lake campground. Climbers use some of them for "bouldering," a sport that allows them to practice their skills on low places that are easier to reach. Three of these boulders at the north end of Jenny Lake Campground even have names: Cutfinger Rock, Falling Ant Slab, and Red Cross Rock.

Jenny Lake itself is named after a Shoshone woman. Jenny and her husband, Richard Leigh, helped the Hayden Expedition when they traveled through this area in the 1870s.

☐ I saw Jenny Lake!

When?

What was it like?

Guess What?

The Jenny Lake area has many old, historic buildings, including the park's first ranger station and a photographer's studio that now serves as the Jenny Lake Visitor Center.

Mount Moran

If you like learning about rocks, Mount Moran is a good teacher. Many stories about the Earth are written on its face.

Mount Moran is mostly made of a rock called gneiss (pronounced NICE). Gneiss formed billions of years ago when pieces of the earth's crust, known as tectonic plates, rammed into each other. Up close, these ancient rocks look striped, kind of like layers of cake and frosting squished together.

The big stripes on Mount Moran are called dikes. The large black dike above Falling Ice Glacier is made of a rock called diabase. When it was molten—hot and liquid, like lava—the diabase squeezed into cracks in the gneiss. Then it cooled and hardened. This dike is 150 feet wide and goes on for miles.

You can also see dikes of lighter-colored granite swirling across the face of Mount Moran. Like diabase, molten granite squeezed into cracks or weak sections of the gneiss. Granite is speckled, and when it is close enough to touch, it probably looks familiar to you. You may have seen it cut and polished in a kitchen counter-top! Granite is very hard. It resists erosion and helps the mountains keep their jagged shape.

Mount Moran still has five small glaciers left from the Little Ice Age: Falling Ice Glacier, Skillet, and Triple.

Guess What?

The small tan patch at Mount Moran's summit is sandstone—left over from a 500-million-year old beach. Long before the mountains started to rise, this area was covered by a shallow sea.

☐ Mount Moran!

When?

What was it like?

Where to see it

From the northern boundary of the park south to **Signal Mountain Lodge**. There are especially nice views from **Jackson Lake Overlook**, **Signal Mountain Summit**, and if you want to hike, **Grandview Point**.

Compared to the Teton Range, Jackson Lake is young. Like Jenny Lake and other lakes at the base of the Tetons, it was dug out by glaciers during the last Ice Age, which ended around 14,000 years ago. Moraines trapped melting ice and snow in the giant hole, and it became a lake.

Before the dam was built in the early 1900s, Jackson Lake was 400 feet deep. With the dam, it is now 39 feet deeper. Can you picture a 40-story building standing in the deepest part of the lake? Its roof would barely peek out of the water.

Jackson Lake has been important to people for many thousands of years. The area's first human residents set up large camps near the lake to hunt, fish, and collect plants like camas. Scientists called archeologists (pronounced AR-key-ol-uh-jists) have found many things they left behind, including spear points, roasting pits, soapstone pots, and weights for fishing nets. One roasting pit is almost 6,000 years old! (If you find any arrowheads or other items, please leave them where they are and tell a ranger.)

You can stop by the Colter Bay Visitor Center to see a display about this area's first people. While you are there, you may also get a chance to watch modern-day Native American artists at work. Today, Jackson Lake and the Teton area are still important to many tribes.

☐ I saw Jackson Lake!

When?

What was it like?

Guess what?

Jackson Lake has 15 islands made of dirt and rock pushed up by glaciers. The biggest is Elk Island.

Snake River

Where to see it

From the park road between **Moose** and **Moran Junction**, and from Moran Junction to the **Jackson Lake Dam**. There is an especially nice view from the **Snake River Overlook**, the scene of a famous photograph by Ansel Adams.

The scariest snake in Grand Teton National Park is not a reptile. It's a river. When snowmelt pours down the mountains in late spring, the Snake River may flow at more than 20,000 cubic feet per second past the measuring station at Moose (the town, not the animal). That means that well over a million pounds of water can be moving past that point each second! You can see why rangers don't recommend swimming in the Snake.

The Snake River is born in Yellowstone National Park and takes a few turns before heading south towards the Tetons. In some places, the river rushes through riffles and rapids. In others, it winds slowly, looping back and forth like ribbon candy. From its source, it travels more than 1,000 miles before it merges with the Columbia River on its way to the Pacific Ocean.

This powerful river's name is the result of a mix-up. White explorers thought a Shoshone hand sign meant "snake." But the Shoshone probably were referring to grass-weaving or fish instead. Can you imagine what that hand sign looked like?

Snake River fine-spotted cutthroat still swim in the river and other streams nearby. This native trout is a close relative of the Yellowstone cutthroat but is covered with much smaller spots on its back and sides—hundreds of them. It's hard to tell different kinds of cutthroats apart, but all of them have reddish-pink slashes under their throats.

Guess what?

Grand Teton National Park has three species of real snakes: the rubber boa, valley garter snake, and wandering garter snake.

☐ I saw the Snake River!

Where?

When?

What was it like?

Oxbow Bend

If you like taking pictures or watching wildlife, you might want to visit Oxbow Bend, especially in the early morning or late evening. When there is no wind, the calm waters of Oxbow Bend reflect Mount Moran like a mirror. But you are likely to find dozens of birds or even a beaver swimming through the mountain's up-side-down reflection. Oxbow Bend is home to a huge variety of wildlife. Here you can see anything from a muskrat to a moose.

Oxbow Bend was created when the Snake River took a shortcut past one of its loops. That horseshoe-shaped loop, cut off from the main current, became an "oxbow lake." Its quiet waters help provide food and habitat for many kinds of plants and animals. Biologists call this kind of variety "diversity," and it's one of the things that makes the park so special.

Watch the water for fish, otters, muskrats, or waterfowl—birds like swans, geese, and ducks. Look

Oxbow Bend with fall colors

overhead and check the trees at water's edge for ospreys and eagles. If you are lucky, you might even spot moose along the shoreline or elk in the meadows. But with so much to see, don't forget to listen. You may hear the flip of a fish, the croak of a great blue heron, or the soft splash of ducks dipping and diving for food.

☐ I saw Oxbow Bend!

When?

What was it like?

Guess what?
Oxbow Bend is very popular with photographers, especially at sunrise. Sometimes there is barely room for another tripod at the edge of the parking lot!

Menor's Ferry

Try to imagine what it was like to cross the Snake River before the bridge was built. The river could be cold, fast, and dangerous. How would people carry their food and belongings? Their children? Would they be willing to pay someone to take them across on a boat?

Bill Menor thought they would. He settled on the west side of the Snake River in the late 1890s to build a ferry and a small store. To cross on his ferry, people paid 50 cents to transport a wagon and 25 cents to transport a horse and rider. Later, they paid one or two dollars to transport a car until the bridge was built in 1927.

The ferry you see now is a copy of the original one. When the pontoons below the ferry are adjusted to the correct angle, the power of moving water drives it across the river. The person operating the ferry doesn't need to paddle or push.

During visiting hours, you can walk inside Menor's cabin to see his store, kitchen, and bedroom. Bill Menor had to work hard to make a living. He also ran a blacksmith's shop, grew a garden, kept animals, cut hay and firewood, and hunted game for meat.

Menor sold his ferry and other property to Maud Noble in 1918. You can visit her cabin and the Chapel of the Transfiguration nearby.

Guess What?
In late summer, park visitors sometimes get a chance to cross the river the old-fashioned way—on the ferry!

☐ I Saw Menor's Ferry!
When?

What was it like?

Even if you have never visited Grand Teton National Park, you may recognize Moulton Barn. Some people say it is the most-photographed barn in the world. You might want to take a picture, too! But please don't enter the barn or other buildings. They are not safe.

Moulton Barn is one of a handful of buildings still left from the community of Grovont, which is now called Mormon Row Historic District. At one time, Grovont included a school, a church, and 33 homesteads. Under a special law called the Homestead Act of 1862, people here and across the West had a chance to own 160 acres if they could live on it and farm it for five years.

At Mormon Row, you can learn about the homesteaders who lived here in the late 1800s and early 1900s. Barns, cabins, chicken coops, and sheds from six homesteads are still standing. But you won't really understand what life was like here unless you visit in winter. The lowest temperature ever recorded in this area (at Moran Junction) was -63 degrees Fahrenheit! With long, hard winters and short summers, farming was not easy.

The homesteaders held parties and dances, and they worked together to build barns and dig ditches. In warmer weather, these ditches brought water to Grovont for crops and families. In winter, the ditches froze and people had to haul water from the river.

☐ I saw Mormon Row/ Moulton Barn!

When?

What was it like?

Guess what?

After a huge flood hit nearby Kelly in 1927, a place called Mud Springs started pumping out enough water to become a year-round water source. Homesteaders called it "Miracle Spring." We know it now as Kelly Warm Springs.

I Met a Park Ranger!

Have you ever wondered what it's like to be a ranger? Rangers who work in the national parks are called park rangers, not forest rangers. You usually find them wearing the National Park Service uniform of green pants and a gray shirt with a brown arrowhead patch on the sleeve. Some rangers have very specialized jobs, but others do a bit of everything. Many of them have special training to help people who are sick, hurt, or lost.

The easiest way to meet a ranger is to stop by a visitor center or attend a ranger-led program. Rangers called interpreters or naturalists lead walks, talks, hikes, and campfire programs that help you learn about everything from bears to glaciers. Ask about programs specially designed for kids. You can find schedules in the park newspaper, at visitor centers, or on the park's website at www.nps.gov/grte.

While traveling through the park, you may run into other kinds of rangers, too. Law enforcement rangers are like police

A ranger leads a program at Mormon Row.

Guess What?

Even though Smokey Bear is the symbol for the U.S. Forest Service, Smokey and National Park Service rangers wear the same style of hats. Rangers call them "flat hats."

☐ **I met a park ranger!**

Ranger's Autograph:

Where:

When:

officers, except that they also manage things like "moose jams"—traffic jams caused when people stop to see moose! Backcountry rangers hike the trails, keep backcountry campsites clean, and sometimes help rescue people. The park also has many other employees that do important work like fighting wildfires, maintaining roads and trails, researching the park's plants and animals, taking care of buildings, and protecting historic sites.

You can have fun learning about the park and different kinds of park jobs while earning a junior ranger badge or patch. Pick up a junior ranger guide at any park visitor center and complete the activities for your age group. When you are finished, bring the booklet back to the visitor center. Who knows? Maybe you will be a park ranger someday!

Rangers can teach you about baby black bears and other park wildife.

Craig Thomas Discovery and Visitor Center

Park ranger's hat

I Took a Hike!

Hiking is a great way to get exercise while exploring parts of the park you can't see from the roads. It also gives you a chance to notice things like flowers, rocks, feathers, tracks, and tiny wildlife like insects and toads.

Before you go, check the weather and read the park newspaper for safety information, including advice on hiking in bear country and carrying bear spray (for adults!). Talk to a ranger if you have questions. Load your pack with water, snacks, rain gear, an extra layer, and a trail map. Visitor centers offer free basic trail maps for the most popular areas, and you can buy more detailed maps at bookstores. While hiking, stay close to your group, check your map at intersections, and make noise so you don't surprise a bear.

If your group hasn't hiked before, start with a short walk or two and work up to longer hikes. The hike from Jenny Lake to Hidden Falls is very popular and only 1.1 miles roundtrip if you ride the shuttle boat across the lake. This trail can be very busy. Here a few other options:

Guess What?
Grand Teton National Park maintains over 220 miles of trails.

Lunch Tree Hill

.5- mile roundtrip starting from Jackson Lake Lodge. This nature trail takes you up a short hill with great views of Jackson Lake and the Tetons—maybe even a

View of Willow Flats from Lunch Tree Hill

☐ **I took a hike!**

Where?

How far did you hike?

What did you see?

moose! John D. Rockefeller, Jr. and his family saw five moose when they picnicked here in 1926. Rockefeller was so inspired by the view that he started buying land and pushing for the creation of Grand Teton National Park.

Leigh Lake

1.8-mile roundtrip from Leigh Lake Trailhead near the north end of Jenny Lake. The trail takes you along String Lake to the south end of Leigh Lake and back (not a loop, though you can make a loop around String Lake is you want a longer hike). If the weather is nice, try dipping your toes in String Lake. But don't leave any food unattended on the shore, as black bears often pass through this area.

Leigh Lake

Lake Creek-Woodland Trail Loop

3-mile loop from the Laurance S. Rockefeller Preserve off the Moose-Wilson Road. This hike takes you along Lake Creek to the edge of Phelps Lake and back along the Woodland Trail. Families with kids six to 12 years old can check out a Nature Explorer's Backpack for the day from the preserve's visitor center.

Swan Lake and Heron Pond

3-mile loop from Colter Bay Visitor Center parking lot. This trail takes you past part of the bay, a pond, and a lake. You may also see animals that live in or near water, like beavers, herons, swans, or moose. The trail crosses plenty of intersections, so don't forget your map.

Trail to Leigh Lake

47

More Things I Saw Checklist

Grand Teton National Park has around 60 species of mammals, over 300 species of birds, more than 1,000 species of plants, and so many special places you could not visit them all in a lifetime. Some of them are described in this book, and you may have already checked them off. But here is a checklist of some other animals and places you may see in the park. There is also a space for writing about things that are not in this book. Good luck and have fun!

Mammals
- [ ] Wolf
- [ ] Red fox
- [ ] River otter
- [ ] Muskrat
- [ ] Badger
- [ ] Marmot
- [ ] Porcupine

Red Fox

Birds
- [ ] White pelican
- [ ] Sandhill crane
- [ ] Canada goose
- [ ] Merganser
- [ ] Chickadee
- [ ] Clark's nutcracker
- [ ] Steller's jay
- [ ] Black-billed magpie
- [ ] Raven
- [ ] Sage grouse

Raven

Wolf

Fish/Reptiles/Amphibians
- [ ] Snake River cutthroat trout
- [ ] Garter snake
- [ ] Boreal toad

CUNNINGHAM CABIN
← HISTORIC SITE

Places
- [ ] Hidden Falls
- [ ] Cunningham Cabin
- [ ] Murie Ranch
- [ ] String Lake
- [ ] Willow Flats
- [ ] Colter Bay
- [ ] Signal Mountain Summit
- [ ] Two Ocean Lake

Two Ocean Lake

Other Things I Saw
- [ ] _____
- [ ] _____
- [ ] _____
- [ ] _____
- [ ] _____
- [ ] _____

Black-Billed Magpie